FROM SEA to SHINING SEA

NEBRASKA

MYRA S. WEATHERLY

Consultants

MELISSA N. MATUSEVICH, PH.D.

Curriculum and Instruction Specialist
Blacksburg, Virginia

MARY JACKSON

Coordinator of Children's and Young Adult Services
Nebraska Library Commission
Lincoln, Nebraska

KAREN WYATT DREVO

Youth Services Librarian
Norfolk Public Library
Norfolk, Nebraska

CHILDREN'S PRESS®

A DIVISION OF SCHOLASTIC INC.

New York • Toronto • London • Auckland • Sydney • Mexico City
New Delhi • Hong Kong • Danbury, Connecticut

Nebraska is a Midwestern state that lies roughly near the center of the United States. It is bordered by South Dakota, Iowa, Missouri, Kansas, Colorado, and Wyoming.

The photograph on the front cover shows Toadstool Park in the Oglala National Grasslands.

Project Editor: Meredith DeSousa
Art Director: Marie O'Neill
Photo Researcher: Marybeth Kavanagh
Design: Robin West, Ox and Company, Inc.
Page 6 map and recipe art: Susan Hunt Yule
All other maps: XNR Productions, Inc.

Library of Congress Cataloging-in-Publication Data

Weatherly, Myra.
    Nebraska / Myra S. Weatherly.
      p. cm. — (From sea to shining sea)
    Includes bibliographical references and index.
    Contents: Introducing the Cornhusker State—The land of Nebraska—Nebraska through history—Governing Nebraska—The people and places of Nebraska.
  ISBN 0-516-22396-8
    1. Nebraska—Juvenile literature. [1. Nebraska.] I. Title. II. Series.

F666.3 .W43 2003
978.2—dc21   2002015255

TABLE of CONTENTS

CHAPTER ONE

INTRODUCING THE CORNHUSKER STATE

Nebraska played an important role in our nation's history. Above, Scotts Bluff National Monument near Gering preserves the memory of pioneers who crossed Nebraska on the Oregon Trail.

Nebraska was not always the bountiful land it is today. Early travelers to Nebraska called the treeless flatlands "the Great American Desert." In 1806, explorer Zebulon Pike described the land as "barren soil, parched and dryed up for eight months in the year." The first settlers faced what seemed like a barren plain unsuitable for agriculture. With no wood or stone for building shelters, they cut grassy chunks of the hard earth into blocks and used them like bricks to build sod houses. They called the sod "Nebraska marble."

In a matter of one hundred years, Nebraska went from sodbusting to high technology. At the beginning of the last century, some Nebraskans still lived in sod houses. By the beginning of the twenty-first century, Nebraska led the world in telecommunications (distant communication). Other technological advances such as modern-day methods of soil conservation and new methods of watering crops have turned

Nebraska's barren lands into an agricultural state that produces enough grain and meat to feed millions.

Before the settlers arrived, Native Americans called the land *Nebrathka*. Nebraska took its name from the Oto Native American name for the Platte River, which runs through the state. *Nebrathka* means "flat water."

Nebraska's nickname, the Cornhusker State, is derived from the nickname for the University of Nebraska athletic team, the Cornhuskers. In 1900, a sportswriter for the *Nebraska State Journal* in Lincoln coined the nickname to refer to the state's chief crop—corn. The term *cornhusker* comes from the method of husking corn by hand, which was common in Nebraska before the invention of husking machinery.

What comes to mind when you think of Nebraska?

❖ Sandhill cranes raining out of the sky along the Platte River in the spring

❖ People strolling through the bluffs at Mitchell Pass in the ruts cut by pioneer wagons

❖ Fans cheering for the University of Nebraska football players

❖ Cowboys and cowgirls demonstrating their skills at the famous Buffalo Bill Rodeo in North Platte

❖ The Homestead Monument of America in Beatrice

Nebraska abounds with natural wonders and significant historic sites. Turn the page to discover the remarkable story of Nebraska.

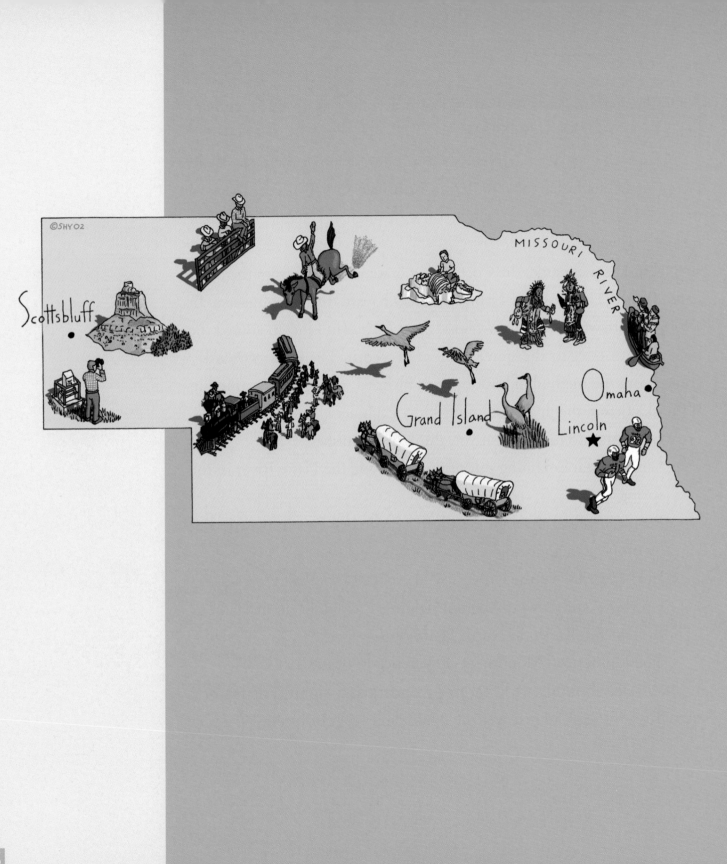

Scottsbluff

MISSOURI RIVER

Grand Island

Omaha

Lincoln

©SHY02

CHAPTER TWO

THE LAND OF NEBRASKA

Nebraska is a state of plenty. As the sixteenth largest state, it shares the products of its soil with the nation and the world. Nine in ten acres (3.6 in 4 hectares) of Nebraska's 77,359 square miles (200,359 square kilometers) of land is used for farming and ranching—more than any other state.

Nebraska is located midway between the Atlantic and Pacific oceans, near the center of the United States. Nebraska's shape is roughly rectangular, with a piece missing from the southwest corner. Six states form Nebraska's borders: South Dakota, Kansas, Missouri, Iowa, Wyoming, and Colorado. The big state of Nebraska covers a land area larger than all of New England. From east to west, Nebraska measures 426 miles (686 kilometers). The distance from north to south is 207 miles (333 km).

The Republican is a slow-moving river that begins in Colorado and makes its way across southern Nebraska.

Miles of prairie create dramatic scenery in Nebraska.

The state's greatest resources are its rich soil and the groundwater beneath it. Groundwater is water that occupies voids, cracks, or other spaces between particles of clay, silt, sand, gravel, or rock within the earth. According to one estimate, if all the water stored as groundwater in Nebraska were removed, it would cover the state with approximately 40 feet (12 meters) of water.

Nebraska is indeed prairie country. However, its lands range from woodlands along the Missouri River to grasslands in the central and western regions to rolling sand hills in the northwest. The eastern third of the state is similar to its neighbors, Iowa and Missouri. The rest of Nebraska physically resembles the high, dry plains of Colorado and Wyoming, its western neighbors. This large state is made up of two major land regions—the Central Lowlands and the Great Plains.

CENTRAL LOWLANDS

The eastern one-fifth of Nebraska, along the Missouri River, lies in the Central Lowlands. The Central Lowlands also extend into the neighboring states of South Dakota, Iowa, Missouri, and Kansas. Thousands of years ago, glaciers (sheets of ice) covered this land. Scientists believe that, at various times during the past one million years, glaciers covered large areas of the earth. These experts think that the last Ice Age occurred 20,000 years ago. At that time, ice sheets pushed down from the North Pole, covering all of what is now New England and much of Canada, Europe, and the midwestern United States. As the glaciers edged slowly forward, they moved rock, soil, and other materials. Later, water from melting glaciers formed lakes, rivers, and streams. In Nebraska's Central Lowlands, the sheets of ice left behind deep deposits of loess—rich, wind-blown soil.

FIND OUT MORE

Today, glaciers cover more than one-tenth of Earth's land surface. Australia is the only continent without glacial ice. One way that scientists study the movement of glaciers is by comparing satellite pictures to track glacier activity. Scientists also drill deep into glaciers and study ice samples to learn what the weather was like years ago. What might cause another ice age?

Soybeans grow on a farm near Falls City in southeast Nebraska.

The Central Lowlands consists of rolling hills crisscrossed by streams and rivers. This area is farm country, and fields of corn, wheat, soybeans, sorghum grain, alfalfa, and other crops blanket the region. These crops flourish in the rich loess-covered soil.

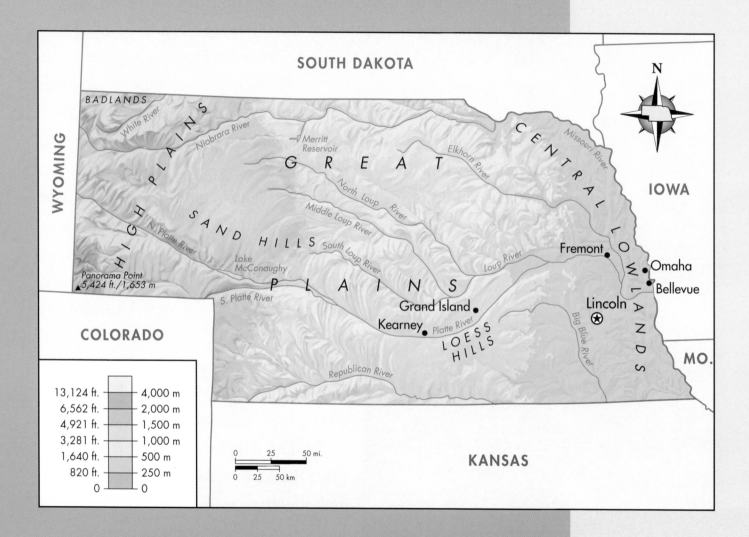

SOUTH DAKOTA

BADLANDS

White River

Niobrara River

Merritt
Reservoir

GREAT

HIGH PLAINS

WYOMING

SAND HILLS

North Loup River

Middle Loup River

Elkhorn River

CENTRAL LOWLANDS

Missouri River

IOWA

N. Platte River

South Loup River

Loup River

Fremont

Omaha

Lake
McConaughy

PLAINS

Bellevue

Panorama Point
5,424 ft./1,653 m

Grand Island

Lincoln

S. Platte River

Kearney

Platte River

LOESS
HILLS

Big Blue River

MO.

COLORADO

Republican River

13,124 ft. — 4,000 m
6,562 ft. — 2,000 m
4,921 ft. — 1,500 m
3,281 ft. — 1,000 m
1,640 ft. — 500 m
820 ft. — 250 m
0 — 0

0   25   50 mi.

0   25   50 km

KANSAS

The other four-fifths of Nebraska lies within the Great Plains. This broad region stretches all the way from Texas to Canada, covering parts of ten states. Much of the surface is fairly level. However, in some places deep canyons and valleys dot the landscape. Loess hills and canyons make up the central and southwestern parts of the Great Plains region of Nebraska. Some of the deposits of windblown soil rise higher than a twenty-story building.

The middle of Nebraska's Great Plains region is called the Sand Hills. This area covers about 20,000 square miles (51,800 sq km), making it the largest area of sand dunes in the United States. This comes as a surprise to those who think of sand dunes as belonging near an ocean or one of the Great Lakes. Thousands of years ago, strong winds blew the dry bed of a huge inland sea eastward, creating hills of fine sand in central Nebraska. Unlike most sand dunes, grasses cover most of the Sand Hills. The wild grasses hold the sand in place. Because of the rich grasses, streams, and abundant well water, ranching is big business in the Sand Hills.

Before settlers arrived, few trees covered Nebraska's land surface. Today, Nebraska has two national forests, Nebraska National Forest and Samuel R. McKelvie National

Although the Sand Hills is generally considered a dry area, some parts of the region contain wetlands, including lakes and marshes.

Forest. Both are in the Sand Hills, and both are man-made. A century ago, a professor at the University of Nebraska thought more settlers would come to the barren Sand Hills if they had an easy supply of lumber. Thousands of Ponderosa Pine seedlings were hand-planted in 1902. The trees grew, but the lumber industry did not develop.

The High Plains—an area of the Great Plains made up of buttes and valleys—lies north and west of the Sand Hills. Some of the hills in the Nebraskan High Plains measure more than 1 mile (1.6 km) above sea level. Because the High Plains receive little rainfall, farmers and ranchers rely on irrigation (an artificial means of supplying water) for growing crops and grazing cattle.

Loess covers the central and south central Great Plains. This region can be rough and hilly. However, the southeastern section is a rich agricultural region, dotted with lakes and streams. This area, which covers about 7,000 square miles (18,130 sq km), is called the Loess Hills.

The block of land extending out from the main area of the state is called the panhandle. Evergreen

The landscape of the Great Plains can be seen from the top of Scotts Bluff National Monument.

EXTRA! EXTRA!

Among the pioneers moving into Nebraska Territory in 1854 was J. Sterling Morton. He and his wife missed the trees of their home in Detroit, Michigan. They quickly planted trees and shrubs around their four-room log cabin, as well as an apple orchard. Morton's enthusiasm for trees led to the founding of Arbor Day—a special day set aside each year for planting trees. In an Arbor Day speech, Morton suggested that we should replant for future generations "as many forests and orchards as we have exhausted and consumed."

In the Badlands region, rocks resembling gigantic toadstools can be seen in Toadstool Park.

trees grow on steep hills in the Pine Ridge area. In the far northwest lie the rugged Badlands—eroded areas of exposed rock formations. Over thousands of years, wind, rain, and snow carved the strange shapes that make up this landscape. Pioneers passed by these unusual land formations on their way west more than a century ago. "One might almost expect to see

Chimney Rock has become one of the most famous natural landmarks in the American West.

smoke or steam jetting from the summit," wrote one pioneer of Chimney Rock, a famous landmark on the Oregon Trail. A steeplelike spire tops the rock that measures about 500 feet (152 m) high.

EXTRA! EXTRA!

While trapping for fur in the Badlands, a trapper by the name of Hiram Scott became ill. His companions deserted him. He died alone in 1828 at the base of a magnificent formation of bluffs along the North Platte River. No one knows the names of his companions, but Hiram Scott's name lives on. The spot where he died bears his name—Scotts Bluff. Scotts Bluff County and the city of Scottsbluff were also named for the fur trapper.

A paleontologist studies fossils of prehistoric animals to find out more about the world in which they lived.

More than nineteen million years before travelers passed through Nebraska, strange animals roamed the northwest plains. Deprived of food during a long drought, hundreds of animals died. They littered the area in and around waterholes with their remains. Over time, the skeletons were buried under silt, sand, and volcanic ash carried by the wind.

For some ten million years, well-preserved skeletons of hundreds of rhinos, three-toed horses, human-sized beavers, saber-toothed tigers, crocodiles, and other prehistoric beasts lay undisturbed. In the 1970s, scientists began excavating, or digging out, the fossil sites. Fossils are remains of prehistoric life preserved in the rocks of Earth's crust. The Agate Fossil Beds in northwest Nebraska and Ashfall Fossil Beds in northeast Nebraska are two of the richest areas of fossil remains in the United States. Bones from the fossil sites have been exhibited around the world.

FIND OUT MORE

Fossils are strange and fascinating records buried within the earth. Excavations are ongoing at the Nebraska sites. Like detectives at the scene of a crime, scientists carefully study the skeletons. What do they learn by observing the bones of ancient mammals?

RIVERS AND LAKES

Nebraska is the only state that lies entirely within the drainage area of the Missouri River, the second longest river in the

United States. It begins in southwestern Montana and flows southeast to join the Mississippi River, the longest river in the United States. The Missouri flows along Nebraska's northern and eastern borders for about 450 miles (724 km). All of Nebraska's 24,000 miles (38,624 km) of rivers and streams drain into the Missouri River.

The joining of the North Platte and South Platte rivers near the city of North Platte forms Nebraska's most important river, the Platte. The Platte River and its two branches cross the entire state, winding east through central Nebraska into the Missouri River. The Platte River is 310 miles (499 km) long, but is too shallow for navigation. Early explorers described the Platte as "a mile wide and an inch deep." However, it is an important source of irrigation, recreation, and electric power production. Other important rivers are the Niobrara, Republican, Big Blue, and Loup. Scenic Niobrara River is home to about ninety waterfalls. The tallest waterfall, more than 75 feet (23 m) high, is found in Smith's Fall State Park.

Nebraska has no large natural lakes. However, hundreds of small natural lakes dot the Sand Hills. Man-made lakes were created by building dams in the rivers. The largest man-made lake is Lake McConaughy in the North Platte River near Ogallala. Ogallala Aquifer, a natural pool of deep underground water forming an underground

Nebraskans enjoy boating, fishing, and other outdoor activities at Lake McConaughy.

water reserve, lies under much of central and southwestern Nebraska. The aquifer provides a valuable source of irrigation.

Nebraskans realize the importance of using their land and water wisely. Dams have been built to control flooding. Today, the pollution of groundwater from fertilizers, insect sprays, and animal waste concerns many people. The state government has taken steps to conserve Nebraska's natural resources.

CLIMATE

Nebraska's climate changes with the seasons. It can be scorching hot in summer, and winter days can be bitterly cold. The average January temperature ranges from about 20° Fahrenheit (about –7° Celsius) in the northeast to about 29° F (about –2° C) in the southwest. Average snowfall ranges from about 20 to 40 inches (51 to 102 centimeters), with the heaviest snows in late winter. Blizzards blow snow across the Cornhusker State.

The average July temperature varies from 78° F (26° C) in south central Nebraska to about 68° F (about 20° C) along the western tip of the state. Tornadoes, thunderstorms, flooding, and

Tornadoes are sometimes called "twisters" because of their rotating, funnel-shaped clouds.

hailstorms are part of the hot summers. A tornado is a dark funnel-shaped cloud made up of violently rotating winds. The collision of warm, humid air from the Gulf of Mexico and cool, dry air from the Rockies and Canada causes an average of about thirty-eight tornadoes each year in Nebraska. The state is part of a larger area dubbed "tornado alley," which extends roughly from the Rocky Mountains to the Appalachians.

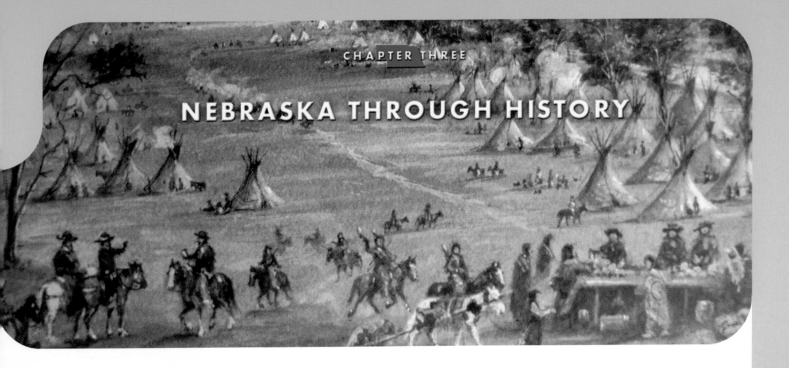

CHAPTER THREE

NEBRASKA THROUGH HISTORY

Native Americans and settlers met at a trading camp near the Platte River in the mid-1800s.

Discoveries of stone tools and weapons have led scientists to believe that people came to Nebraska around 10,000 years ago. These Native Americans roamed the plains, hunting giant bison (buffalo). They ate the flesh and used the hide, or skin, of the animals for clothing and shelter. Over the centuries, different groups came to the area and left. Why these people disappeared remains a mystery.

By around 1200, Native Americans grew squash, beans, corn, and sunflowers. They made pottery as well as bone and shell tools. Gigantic dust storms in the 1400s may have caused them to leave the area.

Over the next few centuries, other Native Americans found their way onto the plains. By the late 1700s, the tribes living in the area included the farming tribes of eastern Nebraska—the Oto, Omaha, Ponca, and Pawnee. These groups lived in permanent earth-lodge villages and cultivated crops. To add to their food supply, they engaged in buffalo hunts.

Western Nebraska became home to the constantly moving Dakota and Cheyenne tribes. These groups lived in skin teepees, which could be dismantled and carried with them as they pursued herds of buffalo. About 40,000 Native Americans lived there in relative peace and cooperation when the first European settlers arrived in Nebraska.

The Omaha Indians lived in earth lodges made of sod.

EUROPEAN EXPLORATION

In 1541, Spanish explorer Francisco Vásquez de Coronado marched north from Mexico, looking for a fabled city of gold. He wrote to the Spanish king that he found only "little villages, and in many of these they do not plant anything and do not have houses except skins and sticks." Coronado and his men returned to Mexico—but not before claiming the entire region, which included Nebraska, for Spain. In 1682, René Robert Cavelier, Sieur de La Salle traveled down the Mississippi River and claimed the same stretch of land for France. Both Spain and France claimed present-day Nebraska.

In 1714, French explorer Etienne Veniard de Bourgmont settled on the Platte River. French fur traders followed him to the region. The Native Americans exchanged valuable animal furs for guns and cooking utensils. Traders then shipped the furs to Europe to be made into clothing.

James Monroe and Robert Livingston signed the Louisiana Purchase agreement on behalf of the United States.

By 1754, Spain, France, and Britain all laid claims to land in North America—ignoring the rights of Native Americans to the land. From 1754 to 1763, France and Britain fought for control of these lands in a war known as the French and Indian War. At the close of the war, France gave up all its claims west of the Mississippi (including Nebraska) to Spain, and east of the Mississippi to Britain. Twelve years later the American Revolution began. As a result of this war, the land east of the Mississippi became part of the United States.

In 1800, Spain returned its land claims to France. Three years later, France sold the territory to the United States. This sale, known as the Louisiana Purchase, doubled the size of the new nation. The United States government stood ready to extend its territory to the Pacific Coast.

In 1804, President Thomas Jefferson sent Meriwether Lewis and William Clark to explore the unknown land that he had bought. Lewis and Clark's band of about forty soldiers and civilians traveled up the eastern edge of Nebraska before continuing west. Their trek westward took them as far as the Pacific Ocean off the coast of modern-day Washington. Along their journey, they came in contact with as many as fifty Native American tribes, most

Lewis and Clark talk with Native Americans during their journey west.

of them peaceful. They also found a land brimming with buffalo, elk, and antelope. Clark remarked that he could see 10,000 buffalo in one glance. They kept a record of the plants and animals they saw. They also wrote of the harsh winters. When they returned to the banks of the Missouri River in September 1806, they had traveled 8,000 miles (12,875 km). Despite the difficulties, their glowing descriptions of the West boosted westward migration and stimulated interest in the fur trade.

MOVING IN

After the Lewis and Clark expedition, many explorers, soldiers, and fur traders passed through the Nebraska wilderness. However, most of them

Bellevue was established as a fur-trading post in 1823.

thought the barren land could never be used for grazing or farming and few stayed. Traders like Manuel Lisa combed the area for buffalo furs and beaver pelts. In 1819, the United States Army built Fort Atkinson, the area's first military post. The soldiers protected fur traders and travelers from hostile Native Americans. The fort, with more than 1,000 people, became the site of Nebraska's first school, library, and brickyard. In 1823, settlers founded Bellevue on the Missouri River—Nebraska's first permanent European settlement. Soon, it became a center for the fur trade.

As settlers and fur traders moved in, Native Americans were pushed out. Native Americans east of the Mississippi resisted the efforts of white settlers to take their homelands. The United States government struggled to find a solution to the problem. In 1830, the Indian Removal Act forced Native Americans to move west of the Mississippi. As a result, the western side of the Mississippi became known as Indian Territory. It included most of present-day Nebraska, Kansas, and Oklahoma. In 1834, the United States government passed a law that made it illegal for settlers to trespass on land reserved for Native Americans.

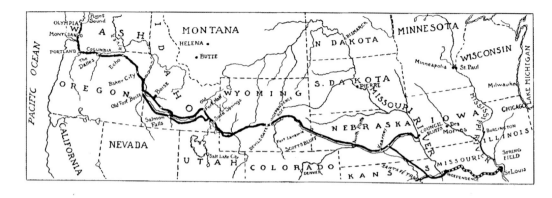

The Oregon Trail covered approximately 2,000 miles (3,200 km) from Independence, Missouri, across the Rocky Mountains.

Although the pioneers could not live in Indian Territory, they could move across it. Long lines of white-canvas-covered wagons creaked across Nebraska on their way to settlements farther west. Thousands of pioneers and gold seekers on their way to Oregon and California used Nebraska as a highway from 1840 to 1860. The route that followed the North Platte and Platte rivers—straight across what is now Nebraska—became the Oregon Trail.

In their diaries, the pioneers wrote of runaway stock, broken axle wheels, illnesses, storms, and fear of attacks by Native Americans. They described the awesome rock formations at Chimney Rock and Scotts Bluff. One traveler wrote of the vast herds of bison: "I could stand on my wagon & see more than 10,000. . . The Plain was perfectly black with them."

Many children traveled on the wagon trains. Much of the time they walked beside the wagons to lighten the loads. Children had regular chores while on the trail. Many herded animals and milked cows, and

FIND OUT MORE

Wagon train travel was slow going. If a wagon train covered a distance of 12 miles (19 km) in a day, how far would the wagon train travel in 20 days?

sometimes drove the ox teams that pulled their wagons. They helped with cooking and washing dishes, and watched after younger children. An important job was hauling water from streams, and gathering firewood and buffalo chips—dried buffalo manure used for campfires when no wood could be found.

With so many chores and so much travel, there was little time for formal schooling on the five-month-long trip. However, they learned a lot from their adventures on the trail. They played, explored, and visited with friends. One child who made the crossing at the age of eight later said, "We just had the time of our lives."

NEBRASKA TERRITORY

Not everyone who traveled the Oregon Trail ended up in Oregon. Some people ignored the law banning settlement and stayed in the wide-open spaces of Nebraska. They urged Congress to establish a Nebraska Territory. There was only one problem: Should the territory be slave or free?

Beginning in the 1620s, thousands of captured Africans were forced onto ships and brought to the Americas. Their captors sold them into slavery to work on large farms called plantations. Plantations were mainly in the South, where plantation owners relied on free slave labor to keep their businesses running. Very few slaves were used in the North, where a mix of agriculture and manufacturing industries employed workers for pay.

By the mid-1800s, the industrial northern states wanted to ban slavery in new territories and new states. The southern states clamored for slavery to be allowed for the sake of the economy. This issue caused tension between North and South. The federal government tried to keep a balance between free and slave states, so that both North and South would have equal representation in Congress.

In 1854, Congress passed the Kansas-Nebraska Act. This law created not one but two new territories—Kansas and Nebraska. The passing of the Kansas-Nebraska Act had far-reaching effects. It set aside the Missouri Compromise of 1820, which had outlawed slavery in the region of the two new territories. The Kansas-Nebraska act gave settlers the right to decide whether or not their territory would allow slavery. Nebraska never banned slavery. However, only a few slaves ever lived there. Permanent residents of Nebraska owned only fifteen slaves during the entire history of the state.

The Kansas-Nebraska Act also helped open the plains to white settlement that, in time, left Native Americans homeless. Eventually, the land that had been guaranteed to the Native Americans became seven states, including Nebraska. This vast territory reached from Kansas to Canada and extended from the Missouri River to the Rocky Mountains. The new town of

This illustration shows a view of Omaha in 1869.

FIND OUT MORE

In 1860, mail service known as the Pony Express began. The horse-and-rider relay system became the most direct means of east-west communications. Young men and boys carried mail packets along the nearly 2,000 miles (3,219 km) between St. Joseph, Missouri, and California. From St. Joseph, this trail followed the Platte River over the Nebraska prairie on its way west. On one of his runs, Johnny Frye, a Pony Express rider, left St. Joseph, at 2:15 P.M. Later that night, at 11:30 P.M., he passed the mail packets on to the next rider. How many hours and minutes did Johnny Frye ride?

Omaha won out over the old town of Bellevue to be the territorial capital. The population of the Nebraska Territory grew from 2,732 in 1854 to 28,841 in 1860.

THE ROAD TO STATEHOOD

Tensions between North and South increased after Abraham Lincoln was elected president of the United States in 1860. Lincoln was against the spread of slavery, and the southern states feared he would try to abolish it altogether. Most Southerners felt strongly that each state should have the right to decide about slavery and other issues, rather than the United States government telling them what to do.

To protect their beliefs, several southern states began to secede, or withdraw from the Union, soon after the 1860 election. They formed a new nation called the Confederate States of America. On April 12, 1861, Confederate soldiers fired on Fort Sumter, a federal fort in South Carolina—the first clash of the Civil War (1861–1865). Although the battles never reached the Nebraska Territory, more than 3,000 Nebraskans fought for the North in the Union army.

While the war raged, Congress passed two laws that boosted settlement in Nebraska and the West. The Homestead Act of 1862 gave 160 acres (65 ha) of land to families—provided they live on the land and farm it for five years. That same year, the Pacific Railroad Act passed. This act called for the building of a transcontinental railroad by way of the Platte Valley. The land rush to Nebraska was about to begin!

Railroads made it easier and faster for settlers to reach the Nebraska Territory. Farmers used the railroads to transport their crops to market. Advertisements of "Free Land!" brought settlers from other states and Europe. Many immigrants came from Germany and Scandinavian countries. Following the Civil War, former soldiers and African-Americans settled in the region.

All these people swelled Nebraska's population to about 120,000—more than the 60,000 needed to qualify for statehood. When Nebraska became the thirty-seventh state on March 1, 1867, the railroad stretched across the state. A special commission selected the village of

Omaha served as an important rail center in the early 1900s.

- Nebraska was the first state to observe Arbor Day in 1872.
- Buffalo Bill Cody produced his first Wild West Show in North Platte in 1883.
- Nebraska was the first state to manufacture and sell Kool-Aid®, invented by Nebraskan Edwin E. Perkins in 1927.
- Nebraska was the first state to complete its part—445 miles (716 km)—of the nation's interstate highway system.
- In 1986, Nebraska held the first governor's race in which both major candidates were women.

Standing Bear's trial was the first step toward limited rights for Native Americans.

Lancaster south of Salt Creek as the new state capital and promptly renamed it Lincoln, after President Abraham Lincoln.

WARFARE WITH THE NATIVE AMERICANS

"If a white man had land, and someone should swindle him, that man would try to get it back, and you would not blame him. Look on me. Take pity on me. . . ." So said Standing Bear, chief of the Ponca, at his trial in Omaha on April 30, 1879. Two years earlier, United States soldiers had forced the Ponca to leave Indian Territory in Nebraska and move to Oklahoma, supposedly to "protect" them from the nomadic Sioux warriors. Standing Bear was arrested when he tried to return to his homeland to bury the remains of his son. After he was set free, Standing Bear became a spokesperson for Native American rights.

In the 1860s and 1870s, farmers, ranchers, and railroad workers took over the homelands of the Native Americans—lands the government had promised would belong to them forever. The government continually broke promises made to the Native Americans. This resulted in years of bloodshed as the natives tried to defend their land and halt white settlement. The Sioux and the Cheyenne swooped through the Platte Valley. They destroyed farms and killed settlers.

The United States Army moved in to protect the settlers, construction workers, and travelers. The military also encouraged hunters to destroy vast herds of bison, the livelihood of many Native Americans.

The discovery of gold in the Black Hills (present-day South Dakota) on Sioux lands created more bloody conflicts. The Sioux considered the Black Hills sacred. They opposed gold seekers looking for gold on their lands—lands in western Nebraska that the U.S. government had promised them "absolute and undisturbed use" forever.

Famous Sioux leader Crazy Horse lost his life in the prolonged struggles. A soldier killed Crazy Horse on the way to a jail cell at Fort Robinson. Other leaders survived and continued the struggle against white settlement. Red Cloud and his Oglala Sioux warriors engaged in a ten-year war that prevented the United States Army from opening a trail to the gold fields in Montana.

The Cheyenne attacked construction workers of the Union Pacific Railroad.

The United States government eventually forced the Sioux to give up most of their claims. Gradually, the violence between Native Americans and whites ended. By 1879, the majority of Nebraska's Native Americans had been sent outside the state, mainly to reservations in Oklahoma.

HOMESTEADING

As Native Americans were forced out, white settlers moved in. The first homestead in Nebraska near Beatrice went to Union army soldier Daniel Freeman from Illinois. He persuaded a local official to register his claim shortly after midnight on January 1, 1863, just minutes after the Homestead Act went into effect.

In the years following the Civil War, more settlers came to Nebraska. By 1870, Nebraska's population had increased four times that of ten years before. The homesteaders faced a harsh and lonely existence. Wood and water were scarce. Lacking trees for lumber, homesteaders cut grassy chunks of hard earth into blocks and built sod houses. Flowers bloomed on the roofs. Photographs show cows on the rooftops. Unwelcome guests, dropping from the ceiling in the soddies, included snakes, worms, and insects. Muddy water leaked into the sod huts after heavy rains.

A family stands outside their soddy on the plains of Nebraska near Coburg.

Natural disasters tested the settlers' survival skills. Between 1856 and 1876, waves of grasshoppers swept across the state. They turned the daytime sky as dark as night. Hoardes of grasshoppers swooped down to feast on the fields of corn and vegetables. The pests not only destroyed crops but also clothing, bedding, curtains, and furniture. At times, masses of grasshoppers covered the railroad tracks, halting trains. Wildfires, tornadoes, and blizzards brought terror to the plains. The blizzard of 1888 took a heavy toll on human and animal life.

By the end of the decade, blizzards and overgrazing had ruined many of Nebraska's ranches. The drought of the 1890s destroyed crops and made for poor harvests. Land prices dropped. Banks and businesses closed. Many farmers left the state. People urged the government to help the hard-pressed farmers. Orator William Jennings Bryan spoke out for giving farmers a larger voice in government.

In 1890, Nebraska's population exceeded one million due to a huge number of European immigrants. By the end of the century, immigrants made up almost half of the state's population. For the new immigrants, work was hard. Men, women, and children often toiled long hours. Many worked on farms. Others found work on railroads, at meat-packing plants, and in factories under conditions far from ideal.

WORLD WAR AND THE GREAT DEPRESSION

Agriculture made a comeback in the early 1900s. Mindful of the droughts in the 1890s, Nebraska farmers set up irrigation systems to improve crop production. Agriculture became more mechanized, saving time and labor. Fenced-in lands kept cattle from straying and helped revive ranching in western Nebraska.

In 1917, the United States entered World War I (1914–1918). More than 47,000 young Nebraskans joined the armed forces. Nebraska's farmers profited from the demand for food to be shipped to war-torn Europe. Wartime demand brought additional land under production.

After the war, agriculture in Nebraska did not fare as well. The economic boom collapsed. Demand decreased and crop prices dropped. At the same time, the cost of production skyrocketed. Not everyone shared the plight of the farmers. By the 1920s, the quality of life for many

Eroding topsoil contributed to the dust clouds in Nebraska during much of the 1930s.

Nebraskans in other lines of work had been improved with the advent of the automobile and electricity.

In 1929, the New York Stock Exchange crashed. This was the start of a difficult economic time called the Great Depression (1929–1939). The depression affected the entire country, including Nebraska. During this time, businesses, banks, and factories closed. People lost jobs because businesses and industries had no money to pay workers. People were left without food, clothing, or homes. Few Nebraskans lost money in the stock market, but the crash caused farm prices to fall even further. Farmers could not sell their crops because no one could afford to buy them.

Farmers suffered disaster after disaster during the years from 1929 to 1939. Drought returned to the plains, causing low yields of crops and severe dust storms. For much of the 1930s, swirling clouds of dust darkened the sky. Many farmers faced loss of their land to banks and insurance companies. The government tried to help Nebraska farmers. Yet more than 60,000 people left the state because of debts, drought, and dust.

The Great Depression gradually came to an end as World War II (1939–1945) began. Nebraska farm products were once again in demand after the United States entered the war in 1941. Nebraska contributed a huge amount of food to the war effort. In addition, more than 128,000 Nebraskans served in the armed forces.

Factories in Hastings and Grand Island made ammunition and weapons. Old Fort Robinson, near Crawford in Nebraska's northwest high country, became a center for training dogs for wartime duties, such as patrolling and guarding installations. Some 14,000 dogs trained in Nebraska. The Martin Bomber Plant near Omaha produced thousands of B-29 bombers, including the Enola Gay, which played an important role in ending the war. Nebraska's flat terrain also made ideal air bases. The government built twelve major airfields in the state. After the war ended, the headquarters of the Strategic Air Command—a force of long range nuclear bombers—set up operations near Omaha.

Nebraska residents also contributed in other ways. The North Platte Canteen began in December 1941. People from several Nebraska communities served snacks, sandwiches, coffee, and other goodies to the servicemen and women who passed through the North Platte train station. The kindness and hospitality of these dedicated volunteers was greatly appreciated by thousands of soldiers.

Agriculture continued to thrive in Nebraska following World War II. Farmers realized they would have to adopt new farming methods in order to continue to farm successfully in Nebraska. They experimented with crops that were more suitable for dry conditions. Wheat and sorghum replaced corn in some areas. Some farmers turned from crop production to raising cattle. The invention of the center-pivot irrigation system put thousands of acres of dry land to use in the 1960s.

Nebraska has helped to improve irrigation technology, which brings water to more than 7 million acres (2,833,000 ha) of land in the state.

Sprinklers on these aboveground water pipes move around a circular field like the hands of a clock. By the mid-1990s, Nebraska had 80,000 wells pumping water from deep underground to feed the sprinklers.

Since the 1950s, Nebraska farms have grown larger in size and fewer in number. The total number of farms dropped from 109,000 in 1950 to about 54,000 in 2000. Modern farm equipment, mechanical irrigation systems, and improved agricultural methods reduced the need for manual farm labor. Many people left rural areas and moved elsewhere to find jobs. While this caused some people to leave the state, others came to the cities seeking jobs. According to the 2000 census, 125,000 more people were living in Nebraska in 2000 than in 1990.

The shift in population to the cities helped Nebraska expand its manufacturing and other industries. Electronic industries moved to the state in the 1980s and 1990s, which helped to offset the flight of farmworkers. However, Nebraska remains primarily an agricultural state with its farm products marketed worldwide. Nebraskans have faced challenges in the past with strength, determination, and creativity. No doubt, they will continue to do so in the future.

CHAPTER FOUR

GOVERNING NEBRASKA

The base of the capitol represents the flat plains of Nebraska, and the tower symbolizes the high hopes and dreams of early pioneers.

Nebraska's government is organized according to its constitution. Every state has a constitution, which outlines the basic laws and rules that run the government. In 1866, Nebraska adopted its first constitution, hastily written, in preparation for statehood. A new one was written and adopted in 1875. Today, Nebraska still operates under the 1875 constitution, though many amendments, or changes, have been added.

In 1920, Nebraska held a constitutional convention, a meeting to discuss the constitution. As a result, 41 amendments, or changes, were made to the document. Another 152 amendments have been adopted since then. The amendments reflect changes in the people's views of government.

Nebraska's government has three branches, or parts: executive, legislative, and judicial. These three branches create a balance of power—

no one branch has more power than any other. These branches govern the state by creating, enforcing, and interpreting the laws.

EXECUTIVE BRANCH

The executive branch enforces Nebraska's laws. The governor is head of the executive branch. He or she represents the state to the nation and the world. Other duties include presenting the budget, or the financial plan that tells how much money the state will spend and on what programs, such as education, health care, roads, or other causes. The governor also promotes new industry and tourism—the business of bringing in visitors—for the state.

The governor has the power to veto, or reject, bills (proposed new laws). In addition, as commander-in-chief of the state militia (armed forces), the governor has the authority to call the Nebraska National Guard to action in defense or relief of the state during emergencies.

Other members of the executive branch include the lieutenant governor, attorney general, secretary of state, treasurer, and auditor. Nebraskans elect the governor and these officers every four years. The governor appoints members of various state agencies, such as natural resources, tourism, quality air control, and health and human resources, to assist in the work of the executive branch.

Many Nebraska governors have lived in the governor's mansion since it was built in 1957.

41

NEBRASKA GOVERNORS

Name	Term	Name	Term
David Butler	1867–1871	Samuel R. McKelvie	1919–1923
William H. James	1871–1873	Charles W. Bryan	1923–1925
Robert W. Furnas	1873–1875	Adam McMullen	1925–1929
Silas Garber	1875–1879	Arthur J. Weaver	1929–1931
Albinus Nance	1879–1883	Charles W. Bryan	1931–1935
James W. Dawes	1883–1887	Robert LeRoy Cochran	1935–1941
John M. Thayer	1887–1891	Dwight Griswold	1941–1947
James E. Boyd	1891	Val Peterson	1947–1953
John M. Thayer	1891–1892	Robert Crosby	1953–1955
James E. Boyd	1892–1893	Victor E. Anderson	1955–1959
Lorenzo Crounse	1893–1895	Ralph Brooks	1959–1960
Silas A. Holcombe	1895–1899	Dwight W. Burney	1960–1961
William A. Poynter	1899–1901	Frank B. Morrison	1961–1967
Charles H. Dietrich	1901	Norbert T. Tiemann	1967–1971
Ezra P. Savage	1901–1903	J. James Exon	1971–1979
John H. Mickey	1903–1907	Charles Thone	1979–1983
George L. Sheldon	1907–1909	Robert Kerrey	1983–1987
Ashton C. Shallenberger	1909–1911	Kay A. Orr	1987–1991
Chester H. Aldrich	1911–1913	Ben Nelson	1991–1999
John H. Morehead	1913–1917	Mike Johanns	1999–
Keith Neville	1917–1919		

NEBRASKA STATE GOVERNMENT

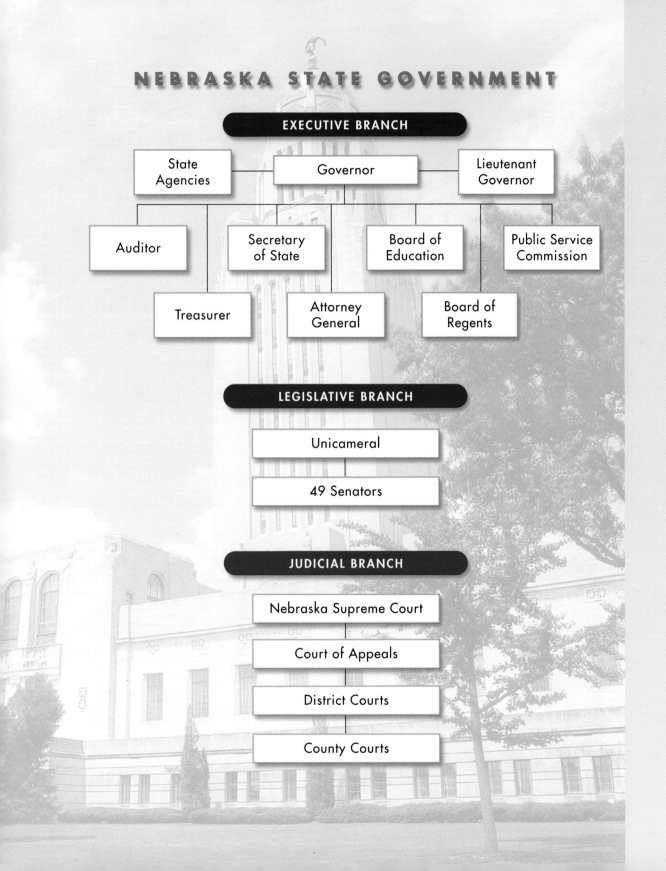

EXECUTIVE BRANCH

State Agencies	Governor	Lieutenant Governor

Auditor	Secretary of State	Board of Education	Public Service Commission

Treasurer	Attorney General	Board of Regents

LEGISLATIVE BRANCH

Unicameral

49 Senators

JUDICIAL BRANCH

Nebraska Supreme Court

Court of Appeals

District Courts

County Courts

LEGISLATIVE BRANCH

The legislative branch, also known as the legislature, makes state laws. Nebraska's legislature is called the Unicameral. While most states have a legislature made up of two houses, or parts—a senate and a house of representatives—Nebraska is unusual in that it has the only unicameral (one-house) legislature in the nation. Nebraska's legislature was not always unicameral. The state had a senate and a house of representatives for sixty-eight years before Nebraskans voted to do away with the house of representatives in 1934.

Today, all of the members of the legislature are senators. The Cornhusker State has the smallest legislative branch in the nation, with forty-nine senators, each serving a term of four years. Each of the state's forty-nine legislative districts serves about 32,200 citizens. The people elect one senator from each district to serve in the Unicameral.

Nebraska State legislators meet in the George W. Norris Legislative Chamber.

Senators propose new laws in the form of bills. A committee made up of members of the Unicameral studies the bills and holds hearings. These hearings are open to citizens. They may speak for or against the bill. After the hearings, the committee votes either to reject the bill, or refer it to the entire legislative body. If the bill passes the legislature, it goes to the governor. The governor may choose to sign the bill, let it become law without his or her signature, or veto (reject) it. However, even if a bill is rejected by the governor, it may still become law if three-fifths of the senators vote to override the governor's veto.

JUDICIAL BRANCH

The judicial branch of Nebraska's government interprets and explains the laws passed by the Unicameral. A system of courts and judges make up the judicial branch. There are different levels of courts—county courts, district courts, a court of appeals, and the state supreme court.

County courts handle cases such as misconduct, traffic violations, divorce cases, adoption proceedings, and civil cases (legal

disagreements between people or organizations). If the county court determines a crime has been committed, court officers turn the person responsible over to the district court to stand trial.

District courts hold trials. Nebraska's twelve judicial districts serve all ninety-three counties of the state. The district courts hear all criminal cases and civil cases involving more than $45,000.

When someone is unhappy with the decision made by one of these courts (a county or district court), he or she may request an appeal. An appeal is when a higher court—the court of appeals—reviews the case to see if any mistakes were made that could change the decision.

The supreme court is Nebraska's most important court. A chief justice (judge) and six associate justices are appointed by the governor. If a case is disputed in the lower courts, the supreme court makes the final decision. It also reviews all cases involving the death penalty, life in prison, or questions regarding Nebraska's state constitution.

State supreme court justices meet in these chambers inside the capitol to make important decisions about Nebraska law.

TRIBAL GOVERNMENTS

Native American tribes are sovereign nations. This means that they are individual nations within the United States, with the right to form and maintain tribal governments. In Nebraska, four groups of Native Americans operate their own democratic form of government. They are the Ponca, Omaha, Santee Sioux, and Winnebago.

Elected tribal councils head the government. The tribal councils have the power to make laws and enforce laws for members living on the reservations. They usually have courts, a police force, and security facilities. Tribal councils can tax tribal members. They also make decisions about civil disputes—disagreements between people and/or businesses—that take place on reservation land. However, United States law enforcement officials handle major crimes that occur on the reservations. Although Native American lands are not officially part of Nebraska, the state government and the councils of the four tribes are committed to working together to improve conditions on the reservations.

TAKE A TOUR OF LINCOLN, THE STATE CAPITAL

In the 1850s, salt basins attracted early settlers to the area of present-day Lincoln in southeast Nebraska. Native Americans scraped up the salt deposits. They used the salt for preserving food. The settlers hoped to mine the salt for commercial purposes. However, salt harvesting never

The Sower is a symbolic reminder that the state government will sow the seeds of good fortune for all Nebraskans.

became big business. During rainy weather, the salt melted back into the ground. Today the salt flats are underwater.

The Nebraska state capitol, known as the "Tower of the Plains," houses the state government. It is Lincoln's most impressive attraction and one of the most beautiful buildings in the world. The 400-foot (122-m) tower with its gold-glazed dome can be seen from 20 miles (32 m) away. The top of the dome features *The Sower*, a large bronze statue of a pioneer hand sowing grain. *The Sower* represents Nebraska's major industry—agriculture.

Construction of the capitol building began in 1922. It was the third capitol to be erected on the same site, so the design allowed some of the old capitol to remain while the new capitol went up in sections around it. The state continued to do business in the existing building while the wings rose on each side. Ten years after groundbreaking, the building was completed. The construction and furnishing of the new capitol cost nearly $10 million. Only a few decades before, the first pioneers had built their homes out of sod. Now a magnificent Indiana limestone building towered over the plains.

The building presents a lesson in history. Buffalo, carved from blocks of limestone on either side of the main entrance, greet visitors to the capitol. Walk inside the building and you will find the story of Nebraska in paintings, murals, and statues. A mosaic called *The Blizzard of 1888* depicts the story of the schoolteacher who saved her students by tying them together during a raging snowstorm. A mural, or wall painting, shows the trial of Standing Bear. Busts of noted

A bas-relief bison sculpture decorates the exterior walls of the capitol.

Nebraskans are mounted in a section of the capitol called the Nebraska Hall of Fame. The honored citizens include U.S. Senator George Norris, Willa Cather, John G. Neihardt, Grace Abbott, Father Edward J. Flanagan, J. Sterling Morton, and Buffalo Bill Cody.

Lincoln offers many more attractions. At the Museum of Nebraska History, you can follow the story of Nebraska from prehistory to modern times. You will also find hands-on stations where you can touch bison fur and bones, pottery tools, and pottery remains.

WHO'S WHO IN NEBRASKA?

John G. Neihardt (1881–1973), sometimes called the Poet of the American West, came to Nebraska as a young child. He was a friend of Native Americans. He based his famous book, *Black Elk Speaks,* on interviews with Black Elk, an Oglala Sioux holy man. Black Elk tells how the destruction of the buffalo, life on the reservations, and corrupt government officials affected his people.

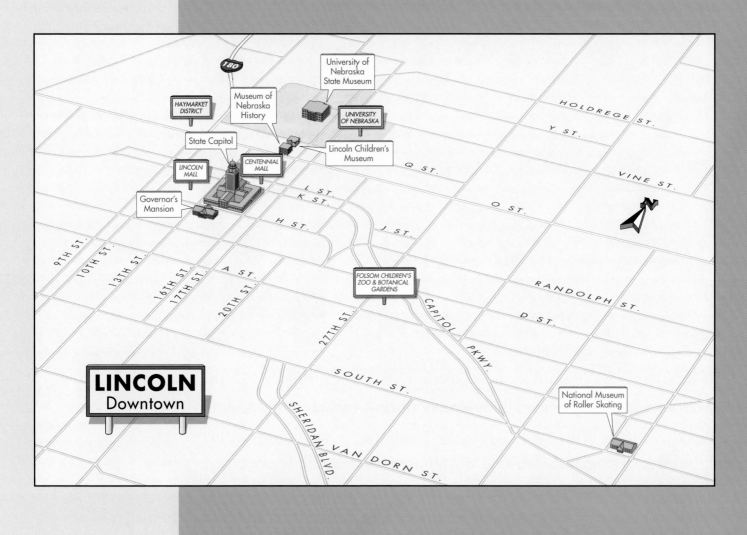

180

University of
Nebraska
State Museum

HAYMARKET
DISTRICT

Museum of
Nebraska
History

UNIVERSITY
OF NEBRASKA

State Capitol

Lincoln Children's
Museum

LINCOLN
MALL

CENTENNIAL
MALL

Governor's
Mansion

HOLDREGE ST.

Y ST.

VINE ST.

Q ST.

L ST.

K ST.

O ST.

H ST.

J ST.

9TH ST.

10TH ST.

13TH ST.

16TH ST.

17TH ST.

20TH ST.

A ST.

27TH ST.

FOLSOM CHILDREN'S
ZOO & BOTANICAL
GARDENS

RANDOLPH ST.

D ST.

CAPITOL PKWY.

SOUTH ST.

LINCOLN
Downtown

National Museum
of Roller Skating

SHERIDAN

VAN DORN ST.

A skeleton of what may be the world's largest elephant stands 14 feet (4 m) tall inside the University of Nebraska State Museum.

The University of Nebraska State Museum includes the world-famous Elephant Hall, featuring one of the world's largest mammoth skeletons nicknamed "Archie." Step back 100 million years as you tour an inland sea complete with the fossil skeletons of giant reptiles and other creatures.

Don't miss Folsom Children's Zoo and Botanical Gardens. The zoo is home to more than three hundred animals, including New Guinea singing dogs. Exhibits have been created to represent natural habitats for the animals—95 species from six different continents. The Botanical Gardens contain 400 plant species exhibited throughout the grounds.

The National Museum of Roller Skating exhibits the largest collection of historical roller skates in the world. You will see patents, medals, trophies, costumes, photographs, artworks, films, and videotapes of the sport dating back to 1819. Interactive exhibits include "How to Build a Roller Skate" and the "Evolution of the Wheel."

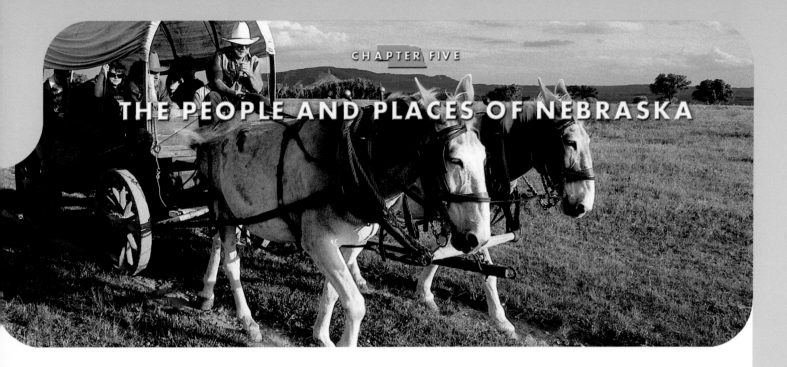

CHAPTER FIVE

THE PEOPLE AND PLACES OF NEBRASKA

Visitors enjoy a covered wagon tour of the Oregon Trail near Bayard.

According to the 2000 census, 1,711,263 people live in Nebraska. Of every 100 Nebraskans, 87 are of European descent, 5 are Hispanic, and 4 are African-American. The state has a small number of Asians and Native Americans.

Nebraska's growing population is centered in large cities and suburban areas. More than half of Nebraska's population lives in or near Omaha and Lincoln. Bellevue and Grand Island are the next largest cities. In contrast, population in the state's rural areas is dwindling. Only 3 in 10 Nebraskans live in rural areas today.

The railroads contributed greatly to the ethnic culture of the state. Union Pacific completed its rail line across Nebraska in 1867, the year of statehood. Other rail lines crisscrossed most of the state by the mid-1880s. To help with the cost of construction, these early railroads received land grants from the government. They then lured settlers to

Children in Clarkson perform a traditional Czech dance.

Nebraska and sold them surplus land at a profit. Many settlers came from other countries. These immigrants brought their families and settled in groups. Between 1870 and 1890, about one million European immigrants—notably Germans, Swedes, Irish, Czechs, and Danes—settled in Nebraska. Descendants of these immigrants make up the majority of Nebraska's population today.

The largest immigrant group to settle in Nebraska were Germans. Beginning in the early 1800s, a massive influx of Germans arrived in the United States, seeking better economic conditions. In the late 1860s, Germans came to Nebraska from other states—Pennsylvania, Wisconsin, Illinois, and Iowa—as well as Germany. Some German-born people who had been living in Russia also settled in Nebraska. Most Germans settled in the northeast region. A few ventured to western Nebraska. They re-created their homeland by establishing their own schools, churches, newspapers, and businesses. German-language newspapers published in Nebraska were read throughout the Midwest.

Swedes also immigrated to Nebraska in large numbers. They became the second largest group of immigrants in the state, settling primarily in the counties of Douglas, Saunders, Phelps, and Polk. Some came directly from Sweden, but the majority moved to Nebraska from Swedish settlements in Illinois.

The Irish were the third largest group to settle in Nebraska. In 1864, Irish construction workers migrated in large numbers to Nebraska from other states as well as their homeland of Ireland. They came to work on the Union Pacific Railroad. For the next several decades, Irishmen constantly flowed into Nebraska. The town of O'Neill bears the nickname "Irish Capital of Nebraska."

Today, most Nebraskans were born in the United States. However, proud Nebraskans across the state continue to celebrate their heritage. Oakland and Stromsburg host Swedish Festivals with traditional dancing and smorgasbord feasting (a variety of foods served buffet style). Dannebrog is the site of the Danish Festival, a celebration enjoyed by families whose ancestors came from Denmark. The German fun-filled fall festivals, called Germanfests, take place in Omaha, Syracuse, and Sydney—and wherever German Americans live. They include German bands, folk dancers, singers, and ethnic foods. The Latino-Hispanic Heritage Festival held in Omaha showcases the cultures of more than twenty countries. Native Americans hold annual powwows. Finally, everyone feels at home during Grand Island's annual Central Nebraska Ethnic Festival, a celebration that presents the sights, sounds, and tastes of the many cultures that make Nebraska unique.

A young Native American dances at a powwow.

Since the time of the early settlers, farming and ranching have been Nebraska's main sources of income. Until recent years, most Nebraskans worked on farms and ranches. Improved farm machinery and modern methods of irrigation have made it possible to produce more crops with fewer laborers.

Nebraska ranks high in national crop production. In 1999, the Cornhusker State led the nation in the production of Great Northern beans, grown in the western part of the state. Nebraska led the nation in 2001 for commercial red meat production. The same year, all dry edible bean production ranked second, and alfalfa meal production ranked third. Corn, sorghum grain production, and pinto beans also ranked third.

A farmer in Carleton transports harvested corn into steel bins for storage.

Winter wheat, grown in southern and western Nebraska; soybeans, grown in eastern Nebraska; and sugar beets, grown in western Nebraska are other major crops. The top cash crop in the state is corn. More than 8 million acres (197,680 ha) of Nebraska's land is used to grow corn.

Because nearly one half of Nebraska is grassland, the state is ideal for cattle ranching. Millions of cattle feed on the grass where

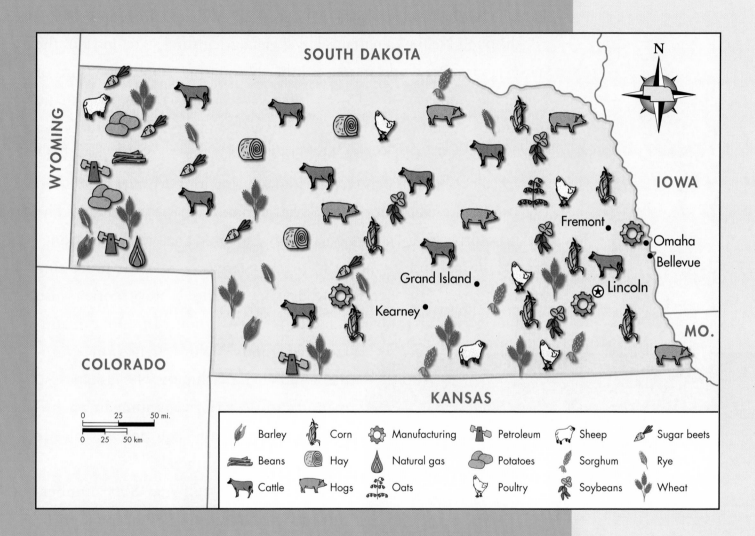

SOUTH DAKOTA

WYOMING

COLORADO

KANSAS

IOWA

MO.

N

Fremont
Grand Island
Kearney
Lincoln
Omaha
Bellevue

0   25   50 mi.
0   25   50 km

Barley
Beans
Cattle
Corn
Hay
Hogs
Manufacturing
Natural gas
Oats
Petroleum
Potatoes
Poultry
Sheep
Sorghum
Soybeans
Sugar beets
Rye
Wheat

buffalo once roamed in the northeastern and north central parts of the state. Nebraska farmers also raise hogs, poultry, dairy cattle, and sheep.

Although Nebraska remains largely an agricultural state, most of the state's labor force works in places other than farms. About one third of Nebraska's nonagricultural work force have manufacturing jobs, many of which depend on Nebraska's farms and ranches. Food processing (the preparing, manufacturing, and packaging of food products) accounts for about one third of manufacturing jobs. Meat products top the list of the state's most important manufactured products. The major meatpacking centers operate in Lincoln, Dakota City, Lexington, Madison, and Fremont. Nebraska's largest center for processing breakfast cereals and livestock feeds is in Omaha. Factory workers also produce frozen foods, baked goods, pasta, and popcorn. Other manufactured goods include irrigation equipment and farm machinery. Nebraskans also manufacture electrical equipment, chemicals, transportation equipment, plastic goods, and primary metals.

Public use of toll-free 800 numbers turned Omaha into the "800 capital of the world" in the 1960s. New companies emerged to answer the many calls for services and information that were advertised on television. The booming information-related businesses created new jobs for

This Nebraskan works at a ham processing factory.

Nebraska grows a lot of corn. The state produces an average of one billion bushels of corn each year, ranking third in the nation. Ask an adult to help make this delicious corn soufflé.

HEATHER'S CORN SOUFFLÉ

6 tablespoons margarine
4 tablespoons sugar
2 tablespoons flour
4 eggs
2 cups frozen corn
1/2 teaspoon salt
1 3/4 cup milk

Here's what to do:

1. Place all ingredients in blender and blend until smooth.
2. Pour into buttered 9x13-inch baking dish.
3. Bake at 325° for 45 minutes or until firm.

telephone operators and for people who serviced the equipment. Today, almost thirty insurance companies, two dozen tele-marketing centers (places that sell products over the phone), and a number of investment firms call Omaha home.

About two thirds of the state's labor force work in service industries. Service industries are those which provide a service rather than produce a product. These include restaurants, health care, schools, government, finance, insurance, and real estate, among other things. The government employs many people in Lincoln and at the United States Strategic Air Command near Omaha. Finance and insurance companies provide workers with jobs in Lincoln. Printing and publishing are also important in the eastern part of the state.

Pilots prepare for a flight from Offutt Air Force Base near Bellevue.

The mining industry in Nebraska includes sand and gravel production along the Platte River. Some eastern counties mine limestone. A few oil wells can be found in the panhandle, but the state does not rank high nationally in oil production.

TAKE A TOUR OF NEBRASKA

From the air, Nebraska's vast plains and flat farmlands look like a patchwork quilt. Today, travelers on Interstate 80 get the same sense of wide-open spaces as did the pioneers. It might surprise you to know that, in addition to its deep-rooted heritage, Nebraska also features a host of top-rated tourist attractions.

Eastern Nebraska

What better place to begin a tour of Nebraska than in Omaha—the gateway for westward migration. Omaha's Henry Doorly Zoo is Nebraska's main attraction. The zoo has been nationally recognized by magazines such as *Time* and *National Geographic.* In addition to 4,500 exotic animals, the zoo features the Lied Jungle rain forest, one of the world's largest indoor rain forests. On your safari, you will encounter the re-created habitats of Asia, Africa, and South America with artificial jungle trees wrapped in vines, blooming orchids, thundering waterfalls, steep cliffs, trickling streams, and eerie caves. At the Walter and Suzanne Scott Kingdom of the Seas Aquarium you can

Several Siberian tigers make their home at the Henry Doorly Zoo.

The Lied Jungle is a re-creation of a tropical rain forest.

view sharks from inside a clear, acrylic underwater tunnel—the largest and longest in the nation. Another interesting attraction is the Desert Dome, which includes a 30-foot (9-m)-tall sand dune. This huge indoor desert re-creates geologic features from around the world.

Omaha's museums offer unique, hands-on learning for people of all ages. Learn about the Omaha, the first Native Americans to settle the area, at the Western Heritage Museum. You can also explore Omaha's role in westward expansion and find out how railroads affected settlement.

If you're a baseball fan, June is the best time to visit Omaha. For more than fifty years, baseball fans have flocked to the city for the biggest sports event of the year—the College World Series. For nine days in June, Omaha hosts more than a quarter million fans who come to watch their favorite teams play at Rosenblatt Stadium.

Not only do Nebraskans love baseball, they also have a passion

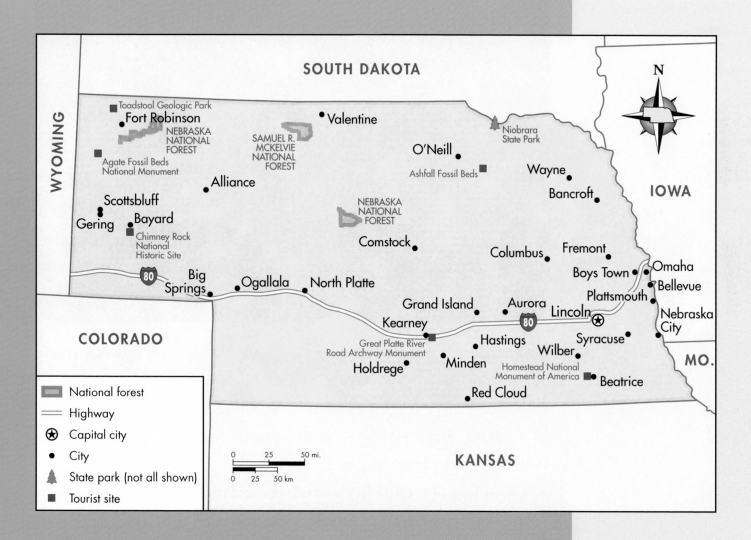

SOUTH DAKOTA

Toadstool Geologic Park
Fort Robinson
NEBRASKA
NATIONAL
FOREST
Agate Fossil Beds
National Monument
Scottsbluff
Gering   Bayard
Chimney Rock
National
Historic Site

SAMUEL R.
MCKELVIE
NATIONAL
FOREST

Valentine

O'Neill

Ashfall Fossil Beds

NEBRASKA
NATIONAL
FOREST

Comstock

Alliance

WYOMING

Niobrara
State Park

Wayne

Bancroft

IOWA

Columbus

Fremont

Boys Town

Omaha

Big
Springs

Ogallala

North Platte

Grand Island

Aurora

Kearney

Lincoln

Plattsmouth

Bellevue

Nebraska
City

COLORADO

Great Platte River
Road Archway Monument

Hastings

Wilber

Syracuse

Minden

Holdrege

Homestead National
Monument of America

Beatrice

Red Cloud

MO.

KANSAS

National forest
Highway
Capital city
City
State park (not all shown)
Tourist site

0   25   50 mi.

0   25   50 km

N

for football. Loyal support for the Huskers reaches from Lincoln, home
of the University of Nebraska team, to remote rural areas. Whenever the
Huskers take to the field, more than 76,000 red-clad fans pack Memor-
ial Stadium. Since 1962, every home game has been a sellout. If you
want to attend a Huskers game, plan ahead.

Other sites of interest in eastern Nebraska include the Village of Boys
Town, the Homestead National Monument of America, and Arbor
Lodge State Park. Boys Town was established in 1917 by a priest named
Father Edward Flanagan to help homeless boys. Located in Boys Town,
Nebraska, this organization continues to help homeless and troubled
boys and girls even today. The Village of Boys Town includes villages, a
farm, churches, and a campus where about 700 children live and attend

Father Flanagan taught classes at Boys Town.

classes. Visit Boys Town Hall of History and the Father Flanagan Historic House to learn more about the dramatic story of Boys Town.

Next, visit the Homestead National Monument of America located on one of the first homesteads, west of the town of Beatrice. The site includes a cabin, a one-room school, and museum exhibits that tell the story of the courageous settlers. Run through the tall prairie grass on the nature trail as pioneer children did long ago.

Stop in Nebraska City for a tour of Arbor Lodge, now a state historical park. In

EXTRA! EXTRA!

For many years, an older boy carrying a younger boy has been the symbol of Boys Town. This symbol grew out of an actual event witnessed by Father Flanagan. One summer day, some of his boys decided to go swimming. One little boy had a brace on his leg and had difficulty walking. Rather than leave him behind, a boy named Jim Edwards picked him up and put him on his back. When Father Flanagan encouraged the other boys to help, Jim said, "He ain't heavy, Father, he's my brother." This symbol captures the spirit of Boys Town, which is loving and helping one another.

1923, the Morton family donated the fifty-two-room mansion, surrounded by a large grove of trees, to the State of Nebraska. It serves as a monument to J. Sterling Morton, politician and tree planter.

Great Plains

Begin your tour of the Great Plains in Aurora, at the Edgerton Explorit Center. The family of inventor Harold "Doc" Edgerton created this hands-on science museum. You can find out about Edgerton's contributions to the field of photography in Strobe Alley, and also learn about other famous inventions.

Moving west, Grand Island is Nebraska's fourth largest city with a population of about 43,000. The Stuhr Museum of the Prairie Pioneers lures many visitors to Grand Island. Walk down the main street of the Stuhr Museum Railroad Town and you will have stepped back a century in time. The museum tells the story of town building in Nebraska. The town depot is in the center of the re-created community. More than sixty original shops, barns, and homes were moved to the site and restored. One of the homes was the birthplace of movie star Henry Fonda.

You can watch a tinsmith in action at Stuhr Museum's Railroad Town, a re-created pioneer community of the 1890s.

For a one-of-a-kind wildlife experience, travel to Grand Island in the spring for the largest gathering of sandhill cranes in the world. About 500,000 cranes land on the sandbars of the Platte River near Grand Island each year. Scientists believe that cranes have been stopping there for the past 10 million years. They rest and gain energy from the fertile lands along the Platte River before journeying on to their northern nesting grounds. Visitors to south central Nebraska can enjoy the symphony of sounds and dancing rituals of the sandhill cranes from mid-February to mid-April. The Wings Over the Platte celebration in Grand Island offers art shows, viewing tours, and workshops.

An escalator in the lobby of the Great Platte River Road Archway Monument leads to a pioneer adventure.

Spring Wing Ding in Clay County celebrates the arrival of other waterfowl. More than ten million ducks and geese use the Platte River for a stopover. The annual two-day event features viewing tours to the local marshes and workshops for adults and children.

In Minden, stop in at Pioneer Village. Twenty-eight buildings house a variety of items that show the progress of our country's development. You can also visit a Pony Express station, a soddy, a fort, and a general store.

In central Nebraska, visit the Great Platte River Road Archway Monument, east of Kearney. The eight-story Archway Monument is as long as a football field and 50 feet (15 m) wide. There you can relive Nebraska's pioneer past and the state's role in the westward expansion of the nation by walking through stunning dioramas. The state-of-the-art audiovisual effects provide unusual experiences such as thunderstorms and lightning.

The town of North Platte lies farther west on I-80. There, you can tour Scouts Rest Ranch, home of Buffalo Bill Cody. From the town of North Platte, follow the North Platte River westward to Scottsbluff—the largest city in the Panhandle. Travelers along this route marvel at the breathtaking sites. These natural sites have remained unchanged since the days the pioneers passed by them in their covered wagons. While you are in the area, check out Toadstool Park and the Agate Fossil Beds. These unusual landscapes and fossil finds attract many visitors each year.

For more spectacular views, stop by the Merritt Reservoir in northern Nebraska. Every August, star gazers from across the country gather there for the Nebraska Star Party. Because this area has some of the darkest skies in the country, it is a perfect place to observe the fantastic summer sky. The reservoir itself has beautiful beaches as well as swimming, boating, and fishing.

NEBRASKA ALMANAC

Statehood date and number: March 1, 1867, the 37th state

State seal: Features a blacksmith, shocks of grain, a settler's cabin, a steamboat, and a steam-powered train. The state motto is displayed on a banner near the top of the seal. Around the outer edge are the words "Great Seal of the State of Nebraska" and "March 1st, 1867." Adopted in 1867.

State flag: Features the Great Seal, imprinted in gold, on a blue field. The banner first flew over a University of Nebraska football game in 1925 but was not officially adopted until 1963.

Geographic center: Custer, 10 miles (16 km) northwest of Broken Bow

Total area/rank: 77,359 square miles (200,359 sq km)/16th

Borders: South Dakota, Kansas, Wyoming, Colorado, Iowa, Missouri

Latitude and longitude: Nebraska is located approximately between 40° 00' and 43° 00' N and 95° 00' and 104° 00' W.

Highest/lowest elevation: Panorama Point in Johnson township, 5,424 feet (1,653 m)/the Missouri River, 840 feet (256 m)

Hottest/coldest temperature: 118° F (48° C) at Geneva on July 15, 1934; at Harrington on July 17, 1936; at Minden on July 24, 1936/–47° F (–44° C) at Camp Clark on February 12, 1899

Land area/rank: 76,878 square miles (199,113 sq km)/15th

Inland water area: 481 square miles (1,246 sq km)

Population/rank (2000 census): 1,711,263/38th

Population of major cities:
- **Omaha:** 390,007
- **Lincoln:** 225,581
- **Bellevue:** 44,382
- **Grand Island:** 42,940

Origin of state name: From the Oto name for the Platte River, *Nebrathka,* or "flat water"

State capital: Lincoln

Counties: 93

State government: 49 senators

Major rivers/lakes: Missouri, Platte, Niobrara/Lake McConaughy

Farm products: Corn, soybeans, wheat, dairy products, eggs, hay, sugar beets, apples

Livestock: Beef cattle, hogs, sheep, poultry

Manufactured products: Processed foods, meatpacking, cereals, beverages, machinery, chemicals, electronic and irrigation equipment, printed materials, metals, plastics

Mining products: Cement, gravel, limestone, petroleum

Bird: Western meadowlark

Flower: Goldenrod

Fossil: Mammoth

Gem: Blue agate

Grass: Little bluestem

Insect: Honey bee

Mammal: White-tailed deer

Motto: "Equality Before the Law"

Nickname: Cornhusker State

Rock: Prairie agate

Song: "Beautiful Nebraska"

Tree: Cottonwood

Wildlife: Antelope, elk, deer, badgers, coyotes, foxes, prairie dogs, raccoons, geese, quail, cranes, bass, catfish, perch, and walleye

TIMELINE

Sieur de La Salle claims the lands west of the Mississippi River, including Nebraska, for France

Lewis and Clark expedition reaches Nebraska

Bellevue becomes the first permanent European settlement

French explorer Etienne Veniard de Bourgmont settles on the Platte River

Nebraska Territory is created by the Kansas-Nebraska Act

Paleo-Indians arrive in Nebraska

U.S. Army builds Fort Atkinson

Indian Removal Act passes

| 10,000-8,000 BC | 1682 | 1714 | 1804 | 1819 | 1823 | 1830 | 1854 |

| 1607 | 1620 | 1776 | 1783 | 1787 | 1812–15 | 1843 | 1846–48 |

The first permanent British settlement at Jamestown, Virginia

American Revolutionary War ends

Pioneers travel West on the Oregon Trail

Pilgrims set up Plymouth colony

U.S. Constitution is written

U.S. fights war with Mexico

U.S. and England fight the War of 1812

American colonies declare independence from England

Nebraska becomes the
37th state

Present state constitution is adopted

J. Sterling Morton
begins the celebration
of Arbor Day

Nebraskans adopt
Unicameral legislature

Kay Orr becomes the
first woman elected
governor of Nebraska

Media tycoon
Ted Turner buys
more than
14,000 acres
(5,666 ha) of
land in Nebraska

Father Edward Flanagan
establishes Boys Town

1867   1872   1875   1917   1934   1986   2000

1861–65   1917–18 1929 1941–45   1950–53   1964 1965–73   1969   1991 1995

U.S. takes part in
World War I

U.S. fights in
World War II

Civil rights laws
passed in the U.S.

U.S. and other nations
fight in Persian Gulf War

U.S. fights in the
Vietnam War

The stock market
crashes and U.S.
enters the Great
Depression

U.S. fights in the
Korean War

Civil War
occurs in the
United States

Neil Armstrong
and Edwin
Aldrin land on
the moon

U.S. space shuttle
docks with Russian
space station

GALLERY OF FAMOUS NEBRASKANS

Grace Abbott

(1878–1939)

Former director of the Children's Bureau. She was internationally honored for her work on behalf of children. Born in Grand Island.

Fred Astaire

(1899–1987)

Legendary dancer, singer, and actor. Born in Omaha.

Max A. Baer

(1909–1959)

Heavyweight boxing champion of the world in 1934. Born in Omaha.

Richard B. Cheney

(1941–)

Began serving as vice president of the United States under President George W. Bush in 2001. Born in Lincoln.

Gerald R. Ford, Jr.

(1913–)

Assumed office of U.S. president (1974–1977) upon resignation of Richard Nixon. Born in Omaha.

Neal Hefti

(1922–)

Trumpet player and composer-arranger of jazz compositions. Wrote background music for *Batman* film. Born in Hastings.

Robert Kerrey

(1943–)

Served as governor of Nebraska (1983–1987) and a United States senator representing Nebraska (1988–2000). Born in Lincoln.

Myra Cohn Livingston

(1926–1996)

Wrote or edited more than eighty books of poetry and other literature for children. Born in Omaha.

Harold Lloyd

(1893–1971)

Popular comic actor in the early 1920s. Known as "The King of Daredevil Comedy." Born in Burchard.

Malcolm X

(1925–1965)

Religious and political leader of civil rights movement, fighting for the rights of African-Americans. He was shot and killed while speaking at a rally in New York City. Born in Omaha.

Mari Sandoz

(1896–1966)

Author and historian. She wrote many books about the landscape and people of the Great Plains. Born near Hay Springs.

GLOSSARY

abolish: to put an end to

aquifer: natural pool of underground water

bison: buffalo

bust: a sculpture showing the head, neck, and shoulders of the subject

constitution: a document that outlines the framework of a government

drought: long period of extreme dryness

economy: the system of making, distributing, and using goods

fossil: remains of animals or plants from long ago

glacier: sheet of ice that moves over land surfaces

homestead: land obtained by living on and farming the tract for a set number of years

immigrant: a person who leaves his or her own country and enters another country to live permanently

irrigation: a system of manmade channels used to provide water for fields and crops

loess: rich, windblown soil left by retreating glaciers

mosaic: a form of decoration made by combining small pieces of colored stone, glass, or other material

orator: a person who does public speaking

reservation: land set aside for Native Americans

satellite: a man-made device moving in orbit around the Earth

slavery: practice of one person owning another person

soddy: house made of blocks of hard earth

sovereign: having the right to make decisions and act accordingly

territory: tract of land

transcontinental: going across a continent

unicameral: one-house legislature

FOR MORE INFORMATION

Web sites

State of Nebraska

http://www.state.ne.us

The official web site for Nebraska.

Governor Mike Johanns Kids' Page

http://gov.nol.org/Johanns/kids/

Activities for children and links to web sites containing information about Nebraska and its government.

Visit Nebraska

http://www.visitnebraska.org

Information about attractions and travel in Nebraska.

Nebraska Blue Book

http://www.unicam.state.ne.us/bluebook

Information about the government of Nebraska.

Solomon Butcher's Pioneer Photographs

http://www.rootsweb.com/~necuster/butcher.html

A gallery of Butcher's photographs.

Nebraskastudies.org

http://www.nebraskastudies.org/

Timelines, historical documents, and facts about Nebraska's history.

Books

Conrad, Pam. *Prairie Visions: The Life and Times of Solomon Butcher*. New York: HarperCollins, 1991.

Stefoff, Rebecca. *Children of the Westward Trail*. Brookfield, CT: The Millbrook Press, 1996.

Warren, Andrea. *Pioneer Girl: Growing Up on the Prairie*. New York: Morrow Junior Books, 1998.

Wills, Charles A. *A Historical Album of Nebraska*. Brookfield, CT: The Millbrook Press, 1995.

Addresses

Office of the Governor

P. O. Box 94848

Lincoln, NE 68509-4848

Nebraska Division of Travel and Tourism

P. O. Box 98907

Lincoln, NE 68509-8907

Greater Omaha Convention and Visitors Bureau

6800 Mercy Road, Suite 202

Omaha, NE 68106

INDEX

ABOUT THE AUTHOR

Myra S. Weatherly writes for children and young adults. Her published work includes *Tennessee* and *South Carolina* in the From Sea to Shining Sea series. She holds a bachelor's degree in English and a master's degree in gifted education. She makes school visits and conducts workshops for teachers and writers. Research for *Nebraska* involved using library resources, surfing the Internet, and talking with Nebraskans. Reading letters and diaries of the pioneers proved to be the most fascinating aspect of the project.